Jesus goes to the Passover

A story from the Bible
specially simplified
for young children

Published by

Bible Society

Illustrations by Kees de Kort

Original Dutch Version © 1979 Netherlands Bible Society,
Hilversum

English text © The British and Foreign Bible Society, 1983

First published 1984. Reprinted 1986.
Published by Bible Society, Stonehill Green, Westlea,
Swindon SN5 7DG, England

SYC 66OP/4   1984   ISBN: 0 564 07133 1

Printed by John Blackburn Ltd.,
Old Run Road, Leeds LS10 2AA.

This book contains:

— the story of Jesus going to the Passover, retold for children.

— background information for both older people and children.

— questions about the story for children to think about by themselves
  or talk about with someone who is older. These questions are
  designed to help children become interested in and to understand
  the Bible story, by relating their own experiences to those of people in the
  story. You can help them to do this by encouraging them to
  think about what it would be like to be a person in the story.

— the text from the Good News Bible. This can be found at the end of the
  illustrated story.

Before reading this book with children it is a good idea if you read
through the background information and the story in the Bible. In this way
you can try to answer the children's questions when you read the
story together.

The material in smaller print is included especially for people who are
going to read this book with younger children.

Background information

Passover is the Israelite festival, on the 14th day of the month Nisan (about 1st April), which celebrates the freeing of the Hebrews from their captivity in Egypt. The Angel of Death killed the first-born in the Egyptian homes, but passed over the Hebrew homes (Exodus 12.23-27). The Jewish name for this festival is Pesach.

Putting branches on the ground was a normal custom at the Festival of Shelters. This Festival is held when all the crops have been harvested, and it helps the Jewish people to remember the time when the Israelites lived in tents in the desert.

In early Israel the donkey was the animal that kings rode on, instead of the horse. They used to refer to the horse as the donkey from abroad!

The Mount of Olives was a hill outside Jerusalem that overlooked the city. It probably had olive groves on it. Gethsemane means a press for making olive oil.

To help you to understand the story

The Passover is a special celebration for all Jewish people. They remember when God rescued them from Egypt when they were slaves. They thank God for helping them and have a special meal. Jewish people still have this special meal once each year.

A prophet is a person who tells other people what God has to say.

Jesus' disciples were twelve people that he called to be his special followers.

Jesus is going to Jerusalem
with his disciples.

On the way,
he calls two of his friends to him.

Jesus says:
"Go on ahead.
Go to that village.
You will find a donkey there
with its foal.
Untie them
and bring them to me.
I need them."

The two friends bring the donkeys to Jesus.
They put their coats on the foal's back.

Jesus sits on a donkey and rides.

Many people see Jesus coming.
They put their coats on the road
in front of him.

Some people cut branches from the trees.
They lay them on the road.
It is like a carpet to ride on.

The people start to sing:
"Jesus is our King.
Praise to our King.
God has sent him.
Praise to God in heaven."

Jesus rides into Jerusalem.
People come out from their homes.
"What's going on?" they ask.
"Who is this?"

"This is Jesus, the prophet,"
others reply.

A few days later the Passover begins.
The disciples ask Jesus:
"Where shall we have our special
Passover meal?"
Jesus tells them where they must go.
The disciples get everything ready
for the feast.
It is evening...

Jesus eats the meal with his disciples.
He says "One of you will help people
to kill me."

They are very upset and shocked.
They each ask: "It isn't me, is it?"

Jesus takes a piece of bread.
He says thank you to God
and breaks the bread.
He shares it with his disciples.

"Take this bread and eat it," he says.
"It is my body.
This is how I give myself to you."

Then he takes a cup of wine,
He says thank you to God.
"All of you must drink some of this,"
he says.
"This is how I give myself to you.
God forgives the wrong things
you have done."

Then they sing a song together
to thank God.
After the meal they go
to the Mount of Olives.

They come to a garden called Gethsemane.
Jesus says to his disciples,
"Stay here and wait.

I want to be alone to pray."

The Triumphant Entry into Jerusalem

As Jesus and his disciples approached Jerusalem, they came to Bethphage at the Mount of Olives. There Jesus sent two of the disciples on ahead with these instructions: ''Go to the village there ahead of you, and at once you will find a donkey tied up with her colt beside her. Untie them and bring them to me. And if anyone says anything, tell him, 'The Master needs them'; and then he will let them go at once.''

This happened in order to make what the prophet had said come true:

''Tell the city of Zion,
  Look, your king is coming to you!
He is humble and rides on a donkey
  and on a colt, the foal of a donkey.''

So the disciples went and did what Jesus had told them to do: they brought the donkey and the colt, threw their cloaks over them, and Jesus got on. A large crowd of people spread their cloaks on the road while others cut branches from the trees and spread them on the road. The crowds walking in front of Jesus and those walking behind began to shout, ''Praise to David's Son! God bless him who comes in the name of the Lord! Praise God!''

When Jesus entered Jerusalem, the whole city was thrown into an uproar. ''Who is he?'' the people asked.

''This is the prophet Jesus, from Nazareth in Galilee,'' the crowds answered.

Matthew 21.1-11

Jesus eats the Passover meal with his disciples

On the first day of the Festival of Unleavened Bread the disciples came to Jesus and asked him, "Where do you want us to get the Passover meal ready for you?"

"Go to a certain man in the city," he said to them, "and tell him: 'The Teacher says, My hour has come; my disciples and I will celebrate the Passover at your house.' "

The disciples did as Jesus had told them and prepared the Passover meal.

When it was evening, Jesus and the twelve disciples sat down to eat. During the meal Jesus said, "I tell you, one of you will betray me."

The disciples were very upset and began to ask him, one after the other, "Surely, Lord, you don't mean me?"

Jesus answered, "One who dips his bread in the dish with me will betray me. The Son of Man will die as the Scriptures say he will, but how terrible for that man who betrays the Son of Man! It would have been better for that man if he had never been born!"

Judas, the traitor, spoke up. "Surely, Teacher, you don't mean me?" he asked. Jesus answered, "So you say."

The Lord's Supper

While they were eating, Jesus took a piece of bread, gave a prayer of thanks, broke it, and gave it to his disciples. "Take and eat it," he said; "this is my body."

Then he took a cup, gave thanks to God, and gave it to them. "Drink it, all of you," he said; "this is my blood, which seals God's covenant, my blood poured out for many for the forgiveness of sins. I tell you, I will never again drink this wine until the day I drink the

new wine with you in my Father's Kingdom."
   Then they sang a hymn and went out to the Mount of Olives.

Jesus prays in Gethsemane

Then Jesus went with his disciples to a place called Gethsemane, and he said to them, "Sit here while I go over there and pray."

Matthew 26.17-30 and 36

Things to think and talk about

Sometimes we have special meals to celebrate, as Jesus did at the Passover.
Do you celebrate with a special meal?
What do you celebrate?
Do you help to get ready for your special meal? How?
What special things happen in your family to celebrate special events like birthdays and Christmas?

Jesus told his friends that one of them was going to hurt him.
Who are your friends?
How would you feel if they hurt you?
Would they still be your friends?

Jesus said that he wanted to be alone to pray.
When are you on your own?
What kind of things do you do?
Do you like to be by yourself?